The Intelligent Quality Investor

How To Invest In The World's Best Companies

Presented by Long Equity

D1528912

Disclaimer

The content of this book is provided for information purposes only. It does not constitute investment, tax or legal advice. It is not to be understood as an invitation or recommendation to buy or sell any of the securities mentioned. The presentation and commentary of investment strategies is not to be understood as an invitation or recommendation to replicate them.

Investments in securities may involve significant market price volatility. The value of investments may go up as well as down. Past performance is not a guide to future performance.

Before any investment decision is taken, if necessary, consult with suitably qualified tax, legal or financial advisors.

Contents

Chapter 1:
Generating Investment Ideas

The investable universe has thousands of listed companies for investors to choose from. Hidden in the investable universe is a small cluster of elusive businesses that share several rare financial characteristics. Such companies can consistently invest their capital at high returns over long time periods, they can raise their prices without losing sales and they are resilient to both competition and economic cycles. Presented in this book are mental models for finding these companies. Mental models are a thought process for allowing complex information to be turned quickly and accurately into actionable insights. They allow for investors to filter the signal from noise and to separate what's important from what's not important. The mental models presented here are focused on understanding the four most important attributes of a company when deciding if it is investable: its growth, its capital allocation, its pricing power and its valuation. These mental models are based on four financial ratios: FCF per share growth, FCF return on capital, FCF margin and FCF yield.

This book is designed to be read in 1 hour. In the course of the next hour, we will cover how to find investment ideas. We will then move on to how to analyse investment ideas, based on four mental models, to ensure that only the best companies have our attention. Finally, we will end with techniques for separating the great companies from those that are just good and constructing a portfolio of high quality investment ideas. Let's get started.

Borrowing ideas from the world's best fund managers

Understanding how something works is a science. If you've ever broken something, just to see if you can put it back together, then you've dabbled in the world of reverse engineering. Reverse engineering is a powerful tool for figuring out what makes something tick. It involves taking something apart, inspecting all individual parts, and then attempting to reassemble what you've taken apart. The process should reveal both how and why something is constructed the way that it is.

Reverse engineering can be applied to investing. For investors starting out, a great exercise is to compile a list of several top performing funds. To understand what has driven their performance you can then look at the companies that each fund holds. You will soon notice something quite interesting. The holdings of many top funds overlap. This means there is often consensus among investors on what is worth investing in. Importantly you can also use this technique to pinpoint where each fund differs to find opportunities that the majority of investors may not have yet spotted.

Today finding the companies that a fund holds is quite straightforward. Funds that hold US companies are required to file a publicly available report each quarter called a 13F. This sets out all of their US holdings, but not their non-US holdings. The international part of their portfolio can be deduced from other documents. Many funds publish monthly factsheets of their top 10 holdings and annual reports of their complete portfolio. These sources can be consolidated to create the complete picture.

To help get you started, the following table covers 10 leading global equity funds focused on high quality businesses. It sets out the overlap between each fund. For example, over 6 of the funds screened held Alphabet, Microsoft and Visa. Funds often trade in and out of positions, so it's helpful to update the list 2 - 4 times a year, so that you always have a source of interesting companies to research.

3	4	5	> 6
ANSYS	Accenture	Amazon	Adobe
Church & Dwight	ADP	Becton Dickinson	Alphabet
Equifax	Danaher	L'Oreal	Autodesk
Experian	Diageo	Paypal	Intuit
Kering	Estee Lauder	SAP	Mastercard
Medtronic	LVMH	Starbucks	Meta Platforms
Moody's	S&P Global	Unilever	Microsoft
Nestle	Zoetis		Nike
Procter & Gamble			Visa
Reckitt Benckiser			
Salesforce			
Stryker			

Looking for what has worked in the past

There's a general consensus in the investing world, and in other fields such as sport, that winners keep on winning. This is often due to a combination of factors, such as competitive strength and a culture of good management focused on the long-term. While it is impossible to directly screen for stocks with these qualitative properties, we can indirectly screen for them by looking for companies that have managed to grow consistently over long periods of time.

The following table sets out a list of US companies that have the highest share price growth rates over both a 30 and 40 year time period (1982-2022 and 1992-2022 respectively). For example, the table shows that Danaher grew its share price at an annualised rate of 23% a year over 4 decades and 20% a year over 3 decades. Each of the companies below have created massive amounts of value for their shareholders. Qualitative research into each of these companies reveals a history of diligent capital allocation and the creation of defensive shields to fend off competition.

Company	40yr CAGR	Company	30yr CAGR
Danaher	23%	Monster Beverage	26%
Home Depot	21%	AAON	24%
Apple	19%	Amphenol	22%
Stryker Corporation	18%	Fair Isaac	22%
Progressive Corp	18%	NVR	21%
Applied Materials	17%	Apple	20%
Thermo Fisher	16%	Americas Carmart	20%
Robert Half	16%	Danaher	20%
Graco	16%	Idexx Laboratories	19%
Gentex	16%	Ross Stores	19%
Lowe's	16%	Cooper Companies	19%
Bio-Rad	15%	Roper Technologies	19%
Nike	15%	Coherent Corp.	19%
Aflac	15%	Gilead Sciences	19%
Valmont	15%	Biogen	19%
Toro	15%	Adobe	19%
Sherwin-Williams	15%	Starbucks	19%
Church & Dwight	15%	Oracle Corporation	19%
KLA Corporation	15%	Old Dominion	18%
RLI	14%	UnitedHealth Group	18%
Jacobs Solutions	14%	CACI International	18%
Nordson Corporation	14%	KLA Corporation	18%
Walmart	14%	Qualcomm	18%
Costco	14%	Jack Henry	18%

No doubt a lot of these names will be familiar to you. But what may surprise you is that a lot of these companies are somewhat mundane. There's evidently a lot of money to be made in paint (Sherwin-Williams), energy drinks (Monster), sports apparel (Nike) and retail (Costco, Walmart, Home Depot).

Such CAGR tables are fairly easy to put together. You will need a spreadsheet that can pull financial data. Next you will need to find a list of companies and their stock tickers. I suggest starting with the S&P 500, before moving on to non-US indices and small/mid cap indices. It's then just a case of pulling the current share price, the historic share price (e.g. 10, 20 or 30 years ago) and then calculating the compound average growth rate (CAGR). The CAGR equation is set out below. Simply input the starting and ending share price and replace n with the number of years between the two share prices.

$$= [(\text{End Value} / \text{Start Value}) \char`^ (1 / n) - 1] * 100\%$$

Linearity and consistent incremental share price growth

A particularly helpful enhancement to the preceding method is the introduction of linear or exponential regression. Don't be scared by these mathematical terms, they are incredibly easy to get your head around.

Knowing that a company grew its share price by 100% over the last 5 years doesn't tell you whether its growth was incremental or occurred rapidly in a short burst. In the following example, both

Company A and B doubled their share price over a 5 year period from $100 to $200. However, the companies took different routes to get there. Company A managed to incrementally increase its share price year-on-year, while Company B's share price remained fairly flat for the first four years and then had a rather rapid growth spurt in the final year.

Company A		Company B	
Year	Share Price ($)	Year	Share Price ($)
0	100	0	100
1	115	1	95
2	132	2	105
3	152	3	104
4	174	4	111
5	200	5	200

In investing, returns can either be consistent or erratic. Company A represents a class of companies often referred to as compounders. They have a long history of being profitable, reinvesting their profits and not being overly impacted by economic downturns. Company B represents companies that are more cyclical, in that they are exposed to economic and business cycles, such as interest rates, employment and commodity prices. Both classes of companies provide opportunities for making money. The focus of this book is very much compounding machines, like Company A, that have high quality underlying businesses, as they lend themselves to less volatile and more predictable investing.

Screening for linear or exponential share price growth over long time periods allows us to locate the companies that have incrementally increased their share price over long time periods. It's not possible to achieve this feat without also experiencing incremental growth in profits. While most data from the financial markets is noisy and meaningless, linearity over a long time period typically reveals high quality businesses that have high quality shareholders. This is because high quality shareholders invest and hold for the long-term due to the quality of the underlying business. Companies mostly owned by high quality shareholders do not see their share price being subjected to wild swings in trading volumes and shorting, which is why the linearity method helps us find them. Linearity is another example of using reverse engineering for finding compounding machines.

Let's consider the linearity of Company A and Company B's share price in the previous example. The measure of linearity is R-Squared (R-Sq for short). A perfectly straight line that's going up has a R-Sq of 1.00 and a perfectly straight line that's going down has a R-Sq of -1.00. Company A has a linearity of 0.99, which is almost perfectly linear growth. Company B has a linearity of 0.73, which is growth, but much more lumpy. When looking at the linearity of share prices, ideally a value above 0.85 over a 10 year time period should be seen as attractive.

Let's look at some real world examples. Between 2012 - 2022 both Stryker Corporation (the replacement joint manufacturer) and Green Plains Inc (the ethanol producer) generated a share price return of around 340%. Where they differ is linearity.

Stryker had a 10 year share price linearity of 0.98, while Green Plains had a linearity of 0.47.

If we look at charts of their share price we can see that between 2012 - 2022 Stryker's share price incrementally grew:

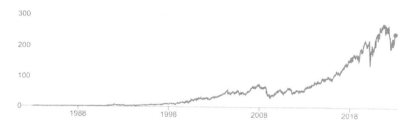

While Green Plains was significantly more cyclical:

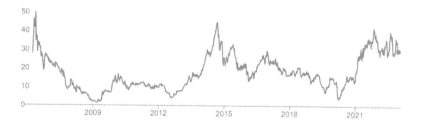

Calculating linearity is a fairly straightforward and fast method for screening for high quality companies. Again, it requires a spreadsheet capable of pulling financial data. You will need share price data at 6 month intervals starting from the current date going back ideally 10 years or more. The correlation function in your spreadsheet will be able to calculate the R-Squared value for you. To help get you started the following table sets out the companies in the S&P 500 that from 2012 - 2022 compounded their share price over 15% per year with a linearity greater than 0.95.

Company	10yr CAGR	10yr Linearity
Humana	24%	0.98
UnitedHealth Group	26%	0.96
Cintas	27%	0.96
Broadridge Financial Solutions	20%	0.97
Broadcom Inc.	32%	0.95
Elevance Health	25%	0.96
Mastercard	22%	0.96
Visa Inc.	19%	0.97
Progressive Corporation	21%	0.96
Centene Corporation	22%	0.96
Domino's	25%	0.95
IDEX Corporation	18%	0.97
Rollins, Inc.	20%	0.96
Waste Management	18%	0.97
Teledyne Technologies	21%	0.96
Aon	18%	0.97
Boston Scientific	24%	0.95
Monster Beverage	20%	0.96
Steris	19%	0.96
Amphenol	18%	0.96
CSX	17%	0.97
Jack Henry & Associates	17%	0.97
Stryker Corporation	16%	0.98
Texas Instruments	20%	0.95

Competitors and duopolies

The last technique we will consider relates to competitors and duopolies. A duopoly is where two companies together dominate a particular market. The application of this technique in investing is simple. Everytime you come across a company you like, look for companies operating a similar business.

This technique can involve looking for similar companies in different markets. For example, the largest e-commerce business in North America is Amazon.com. If you decide that you like the e-commerce business model, you may look for similar e-commerce opportunities in other countries such as JD.com, the largest e-commerce company in China, and Mercado Libre, the largest e-commerce company in Central and South America.

This technique can also involve looking for similar companies in the same market. There are many examples of duopolies that provide similar products and services in the same market. While they are direct competitors, their co-existence often strengthens the other by forcing innovation. Like a monopoly, duopolies often enjoy high barriers to entry. As an investor you can treat duopolies as a monopoly, by buying both for your portfolio. Set out below is a list of duopolies that enjoy strong market positions and are worth researching further. Some will be familiar and some perhaps less so.

− S&P Global and Moody's (credit rating agencies)

− Visa and Marketcard (credit card companies)

− Coca Cola and Pepsico (soft drink companies)

- L'Oreal and Estee Lauder (cosmetic companies)

- Cadence Design Systems and Synopsys (semiconductor design software)

- Fisher & Paykel Healthcare and Resmed (healthcare companies specialised in respiratory disease)

- Sonova and Cochlear (healthcare companies specialised in hearing loss)

- Automatic Data Processing and Paychex (payroll service providers)

- IDEXX and Zoetis (veterinary testing companies)

Moving from external to internal

The previously discussed techniques are all external to what's actually happening inside a company. Use the previously discussed techniques to create a shortlist of companies to research further. The rest of this book can be used to focus on analysing and assessing what's actually happening inside a company.

Chapter 2:
Free Cash Flow Per Share Growth

Having looked at how we can generate investment ideas, we now turn to evaluating those investment ideas.

The best financial metric for measuring growth

As investors we want our investments to grow. Therefore the companies we invest in also need to grow. But exactly what part of a company needs to grow? You could go to a company's balance sheet to look at the growth of its assets and equity. Or you could go to the company's income statement to look at the growth of its revenues and net income. But there's another option.

Free cash flow per share growth

In the view of many investors and companies, the best metric for evaluating growth is free cash flow per share. As net income is an accounting metric, it is open to the discretion of accountants and managers on how it is reported. In contrast, free cash flow is the money that has actually entered and left the company over the accounting period. As free cash flow (often abbreviated to FCF) is a lot harder to manipulate, it is more suitable for measuring growth.

A company's free cash flow can only be used for specific purposes. These are:

- Reinvesting in the company's growth

- Paying down debt

- Paying out dividend

- Buying other companies

- Buying back the company's own shares

A lot of companies, especially early stage ones, provide their employees with stock-based compensation (SBC). While great for incentivising staff and retaining talent, this has the effect of diluting a shareholder's equity. To account for this it is important that FCF per share is used as it provides a more reliable metric of growth.

Rich Templeton, the CEO of the semiconductor company Texas Instruments, says that "the best measure to judge a company's performance over time is growth of free cash flow per share". It's his view that FCF per share growth is what "drives long-term value" for shareholders. Similarly Jeff Bezo, the Amazon CEO, is of the view that "it's the absolute dollar free cash flow per share that you want to maximise". Academic studies have shown that companies that convert a high percentage of their earnings into FCF outperform the companies that convert a low percentage of earnings into FCF. Therefore all businesses, regardless of their sector and the products and services they sell, should be judged as being in the free cash flow generating business.

Long-term FCF per share growth

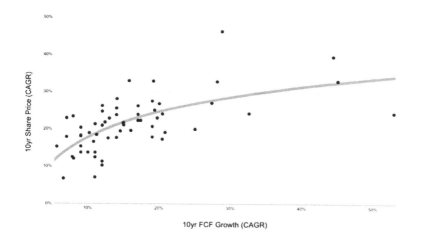

10yr FCF Growth (CAGR)

For the purposes of evaluating a company, it is important to understand a company's FCF growth over a long time period, ideally 10+ years. The above chart sets out the relationship between share price growth and FCF growth over a 10 year period for a selection of high quality companies, suggesting a correlation between the two.

Like we did earlier, we can also employ linear and exponential regression analysis to FCF per share growth to help us identify the companies that have consistently grown their FCF over long time periods with low levels of volatility. This approach helps us remove companies where growth has been cyclical, meaning we can instead focus on long-term, low volatility growth. The following table sets out a list of companies that have enjoyed both high and linear FCF growth between 2012 - 2022.

Company	10yr FCF CAGR	Linearity
Verisign	9%	0.98
Qualys	27%	0.97
Texas Instruments	10%	0.97
Paycom	42%	0.97
Aspen Tech	14%	0.97
Factset	11%	0.97
Constellation Software	28%	0.96
Mastercard	15%	0.96
Novo Nordisk	10%	0.95
Paychex	9%	0.95
Descartes Systems	20%	0.95
Amazon	53%	0.95
Nemetschek	19%	0.95
MSCI	16%	0.94
Adobe	19%	0.94
Diasorin	14%	0.94
Expeditors International	12%	0.94
Zoetis	19%	0.94
L'Oreal	8%	0.93
S&P Global	21%	0.93
Veeva Systems	34%	0.93
Mettler Toledo	17%	0.93

Intuit	12%	0.93
NVIDIA	29%	0.92
Cadence Design Systems	14%	0.92
Visa	15%	0.91
Zebra Technologies	20%	0.91
ADP	6%	0.91
IDEXX	17%	0.90
TechnologyOne	15%	0.90

Mastercard, the payment processing company, is a great example of a company that has consistently grown its FCF per share over a long period of time. Since 2006, Mastercard has grown its FCF at an average rate of 23% per year. The following chart demonstrates just how consistent this growth has been. Applying an exponential regression to the data reveals a R-Sq value of 0.96, which is about as close to a perfect line of best fit that you can get from real world data.

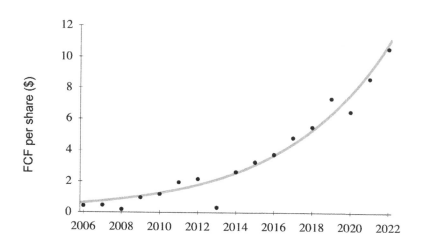

Where FCF growth has gone, share price has followed. Over the same time period the company's share price has grown by 31% per year. The fact that Mastercard's share price growth (31%) outpaced its FCF growth (23%) over this time period is due to the company's valuation also increasing at the same time, thus providing an additional boost to the share price. This topic will be revisited in a later chapter.

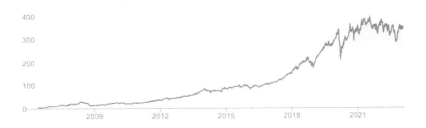

FCF per share growth alone is not enough

Determining a company's FCF growth is only the first step in our analysis. We now need to reach a view on whether growth can be maintained into the future. To retain and reinvest profits for growth, a company needs to have opportunities for future growth. It's therefore important to understand the trends that produced the growth in the past and to reach a view on whether that can continue. Such growth may come from an increase in prices, creating and selling new products, or selling existing products in new markets. How future-proof a company's growth is, is best supported by evidence that the company can allocate capital efficiently, add value to its supply chain and shield itself from competition. These will be the subjects of the following chapters.

Chapter 3:
Compounding Capital

The capital lifecycle

Companies need capital. This is essentially money, but in the context of corporate finance it takes two forms: debt and equity. In the context of financial markets, these two forms of capital are known as bonds (debt) and shares (equity). When a company needs money, it issues one or both of these types of capital.

Once it has its money, the company then engages with its supply chain. Companies have suppliers of goods and services, and they are also the suppliers of goods and services to their customers. The lifecycle of a company's capital is therefore as follows. A business will:

1. Borrow money from their debt and equity investors,

2. Exchange the money with their suppliers for goods and services,

3. Provide goods and services to their customers in exchange for payment, then

4. Return surplus profits to their investors.

The three rules of corporate finance

Corporate finance is the area of finance that concerns: (i) how a company funds itself (i.e. how it raises capital), and (ii) how it invests its capital. The primary goal of corporate finance is to maximise the value of the company. This is achieved by following the three rules of corporate finance:

1. Buy high returning assets.

2. Use low cost debt to finance the purchase of high returning assets.

3. Only return capital to investors if there are no suitable opportunities for reinvestment.

The rules of corporate finance have two implications for investors. Firstly, like companies, our aim when buying investments should also be maximising total return. This means we should not limit ourselves to one region of the world or one sector or industry. Instead we should only focus on investing in high quality assets with good opportunities for high returns. Secondly, when we evaluate a company we should consider (i) how high the return is on their assets, (ii) how low the cost is of their debt, and (iii) their framework for returning capital to investors.

Return on capital

The best starting place for understanding how diligent a company is when it comes to corporate finance is to look at its return on capital (ROC). ROC is a measure of the return a company generates from the capital it has invested, thus revealing how effective it is at using the capital it has raised from investors.

There are several ways to calculate the return on capital. A common way is to calculate the return on its equity capital. This essentially means comparing a company's income statement with its balance sheet by calculating net income as a percentage of shareholder equity. There are two shortcomings to this method. In terms of the numerator of the equation, we have already seen that net income is an accounting metric, which is open to discretion in how accountants and managers report it. In terms of the denominator part of the equation, shareholder equity can also be distorted if large amounts of debt are used to boost a company's returns. Therefore, the ideal return on capital metric should reflect the amount of cash returned for every dollar of capital invested into the business. In summary, the preferred approach is to calculate the company's free cash flow return on its invested capital (the sum of a company's shareholder equity and non-current liabilities). Once expressed as a percentage, the number tells you how many dollars of cash the company generates for every $100 of capital invested.

Value creation

A company's return on capital must be higher than its cost of capital. If a company can borrow capital at around 2% and can invest it at a return of 20%, then over time the company is creating a value. If a company borrows capital at 7% and can only generate a return of 3%, then over time it is destroying value.

While a high return on capital implies that a company is both profitable and using its debt efficiently, it is also important to consider how much debt capital to equity capital is being used to finance the company. This is known as leverage. The less debt a company has on its balance sheet, the less leveraged it is. Analysis of a company's debt can also be further understood by looking at its interest coverage, which measures how easily a company can pay interest on its debt.

The MSCI World Quality Index consists of companies that have high returns on capital. From 1994 - 2022 this quality-focused index returned 11.08%, while the benchmark, the MSCI World Index, only returned 7.76%. Over the last 25 years, there has not been a single 10 year period when the quality index didn't outperform its benchmark. Similarly, Morgan Stanley's paper "The Equity Compounders" showed that the constituents of the MSCI Europe Index with the highest returns on capital over the long-term consistently outperform those with the lowest returns on capital. If you want to outperform, then it clearly makes sense to consider the return on capital.

Defying economic gravity

While a high return on capital is great, a consistently high value over a long period of time is even better. A lot can be inferred from a company that is able to maintain a high return on capital for a long time. Not only does it signal that the company is an efficient capital allocator and can use the capital it raises effectively, it also suggests that the company has advantages over its competition.

The economic law of mean reversion suggests that a company with a high return on capital should see competitors infiltrate its market, offer a cheaper and/or better alternative and thus compete away its high returns on capital. We can infer that the small number of companies that defy economic gravity and maintain a high return on capital over a long time period benefit from competitive advantages. The following table sets out the companies that have managed to average a free cash flow return on capital above 15% over the last 10 years. Research into the business models of these companies reveals that often they enjoy a combination of intangible advantages (such as a strong brand and intellectual property) in addition to cost advantages (they can produce what they sell at a lower cost than their competitors), switching costs (there's a cost or inconvenience in finding a replacement which incentivises their customers to stay) and network effects (meaning that their product improves as more people use it, thus creating a snowball effect).

Company	10yr average FCF ROC
Verisign	76%
Novo Nordisk	60%
Intuit	51%
Constellation Software	44%
Mastercard	40%
TechnologyOne	37%
Paychex	36%
IDEXX	36%
Qualys	35%
Factset	34%
Texas Instruments	29%
S&P Global	27%
Veeva Systems	26%
Nemetschek	25%
Cadence Design Systems	25%
Mettler Toledo	24%
Expeditors International	24%
Moodys	23%
Diasorin	23%
Automatic Data Processing	23%
Adobe	22%
KLA	21%
Microsoft	21%
NVIDIA	20%
Alphabet	17%
Paycom	17%
ASML	17%
Edwards Lifesciences	16%
Visa	16%
MSCI	16%
Zebra Technologies	15%

As you will have noticed, there aren't any banks, airlines or energy companies in the above list, as such sectors don't lend themselves to the long-term growth of free cash flow. Instead the above companies are mostly in the tech and healthcare sectors, and predominantly provide services to other businesses rather than directly to consumers. The following table sets out the average returns on capital for a small selection of sectors. Typically it is the technology, healthcare and consumer sectors that generate the highest returns on capital, while the more cyclical airlines, banks and energy companies generate lower returns.

Sector	Average ROC	Sector	Average ROC
Consumer staples	35%	Airlines	-16%
Healthcare	35%	Banks	-0.1%
Software	22%	Oil companies	-6%

These cross-sector differences in returns on capital are reflected in share price performance. The following table sets out the annualised total return (share price return plus dividend income) from 1994 - 2022 for a range of industries and sectors.

Sector	Annualised Total Return (1994 - 2022)
Software	12.9%
Healthcare	11.1%
Household/personal items	10.0%
Energy	8.9%
Benchmark	7.8%
Transport	7.2%
Communication services	5.1%
Automobiles	4.9%
Banks	4.5%

The sectors with low returns on capital are often exposed to interest rates (e.g. banks), commodity prices (e.g. fuel for airlines, oil for energy companies), the economic cycle (the demand for recreational travel drops during a recession) and competitors (e.g. there are hundreds of banks compared to just two major credit card companies). In contrast, sectors with high returns on capital see consistent demand for their products, even during an economic slump, they are not overly exposed to interest rates or commodity prices, and exist in sectors where it's easier to create and maintain competitive advantages.

Compounding capital

Being able to maintain a high return on capital over a long period of time links directly to the previous chapter on the importance of a high growth rate. If a company is able to maintain a return on capital of 20% over a 10 year period, like the chip manufacturer NVIDIA managed to do from 2012 - 2022, then in their first year they will generate a return of $20 for every $100 of capital they invest into the business. The following table sets out what a return on capital of 20% looks like over a 10 year time period. Assuming they decide to retain the $20 of profit as capital, the following year they will have $120 to invest. If they can invest that $120 and generate another 20% return, then at the end of the second year they would have made $24 and will have $144 to invest for the following year. This is the power of compounding as they are not only generating returns on the original capital, they are growing their capital and making returns on their retained and reinvested profits. Maintaining a 20% ROC means that overtime both the amount of invested capital and the return generated will compound in value.

Year	Capital	Return	ROC
0	$100		20%
1	$120	$20	20%
2	$144	$24	20%
3	$173	$29	20%
4	$207	$35	20%
5	$249	$41	20%
6	$299	$50	20%
7	$358	$60	20%
8	$430	$72	20%
9	$516	$86	20%
10	$619	$103	20%

In the above example the hypothetical company retains 100% of its profits, meaning that the $20 return made in year 1 is retained and reinvested as capital in year 2. In reality, most companies will return at least some of their profits to shareholders. A company's payout ratio is the percentage of its profits that a company returns to its shareholders in the form of a dividend. It's important to be mindful of this ratio when looking for high quality compounders, as a high and increasing payout suggests that the company lacks growth opportunities. It's also important to be mindful that a company can use payouts to keep its capital at a low level and therefore its return on capital at a high level. Such companies are typically evidenced by a high return on capital and a low FCF growth rate. For long-term compounding it's important that both high growth and a high ROC be in place.

An example of this is set out in the following table. The bleach company, Clorox, and the semiconductor companies, Texas Instruments and NVIDIA, all have similar returns on capital. However, Clorox pays significantly more of its earnings out as a dividend. The consequence is that Clorox has a significantly lower FCF growth rate than the semiconductor companies. We can infer that the reason for Clorox's high payout ratio is due to a lack of reinvestment opportunities, which the semiconductor companies are not currently experiencing.

Year	Clorox	Texas Instruments	NVIDIA
10yr avg. ROC	25%	26%	22%
10yr avg. payout	69%	53%	19%
10yr FCF CAGR	2%	10%	27%

One option for investors faced with a company that has a high return on capital, but also a high payout ratio, is to reinvest the dividends by purchasing more shares in the company. This isn't ideal, as having the company reinvest its capital for you saves on transaction fees and taxes. Investors will also benefit from the price-to-book (P/B) ratio. If a company has a P/B ratio of 10, then that effectively means it costs $10 to buy just $1 of a company's capital. This is inefficient for investors looking to reinvest dividends, but very efficient for investors in companies that reinvest earnings, rather than paying them out. This is because if a company retains $1 of earnings, then that $1 of earnings has a market value of $10.

Chapter 4:
Pricing Power

Free cash flow margins

Companies have two key relationships. An effective relationship with their investors is reflected in a consistently high return on capital (covered in the previous chapter). An effective relationship with their supply chain is reflected in a consistently high margin. Companies buy raw materials and pay for services, they then add value to what they take in and sell to customers their value-added products.

Just like return on capital, there are several ways to calculate a company's margin. They all start with a company's revenue, which is the total amount of income a company generates from the sale of its goods and services.

The gross profit margin is calculated by taking gross profit as a percentage of revenue. If a company generates $10bn in revenue and $6bn in gross profit, then the company has a gross profit margin of 60%. This means that the company makes things for

$4 and sells them for $10. It's obviously better to be able to make something for $4 and sell it for $10, than it would be to make something for $8 and sell it for $10.

Morningstar's paper titled "Not All Moats Are Created Equal" categorises the strength of a company's competitive advantage as either having a wide moat, a narrow moat or a narrow moat. They demonstrated that wide moat companies (those with the strongest competitive advantages) have the highest returns on capital, the highest margins and consequently the highest long-term share price return. In contrast, no moat companies (those without competitive advantages) have the lowest returns on capital, the lowest margins and consequently the lowest share price return.

Pricing power and inflation

Like net income, gross profit has the potential to be adjusted by accountants. Therefore, free cash flow is the preferred numerator when calculating margins. The FCF margin is a company's free cash flow divided by its revenue and expressed as a percentage. It is the measure of the amount of cash generated by a company as a proportion of its revenue. Ultimately the FCF margin indicates the amount of value a company is creating for its supply chain. A consistently high FCF margin sustained over a long time period is the best indicator that a company has pricing power. An increasing margin over time indicates that a company's pricing power is strengthening.

The best protection against inflation is to own companies that have pricing power. As investors we want companies that are price setters, not price takers. Oil companies are ultimately price takers, as they can't control the price of oil, which is set externally by the global oil market. Companies with pricing power are price setters. They are typically insulated from commodity prices and interest rates, and can consistently raise their prices over time, often above inflation, without seeing a decrease in demand for their product. When inflation climbs, companies with pricing power are able to pass on their increased costs to their customers.

Both interest rates and inflation can cause investors concern. If a company has a high return on capital, then the fact that it can generate large returns in proportion to its capital means it can protect itself from interest rate shocks. Similarly, if a company has a high margin, then the fact that it can consistently increase its prices above inflation, means that it should be in a position to withstand an inflation shock and pass on increased costs to its customers.

Business models

As we have already seen, the long-term compounding of capital requires consistent FCF growth. This is the result of a company being able to retain and reinvest its profits, ideally at high returns on capital, over long periods of time. As inflation and interest rates will inevitably change over a long period of time, it's important to look for companies that can protect themselves against economic shocks, and therefore have high margins. The following table is a list of companies that have managed to maintain a very high average FCF margin over a 10 year period. You will notice only a small number of sectors are able to maintain high margins. They typically include companies that sell software, semiconductors, payment services, credit ratings, financial exchanges, healthcare and luxury items.

Company	10yr average FCF Margin
Verisign	56%
Visa	46%
Mastercard	42%
Aspen Tech	41%
MarketAxess	40%
MSCI	35%
Adobe	34%
ANSYS	34%
London Stock Exchange	32%
Intercontinental Exchange	32%
Texas Instruments	32%
Microsoft	31%
Novo Nordisk	31%
Intuit	31%
Paychex	30%
Descartes Systems	30%
Moodys	30%
Analog Devices	29%
Qualys	29%
Veeva Systems	28%
S&P Global	27%
KLA	27%
Factset	27%
Hermes	25%
NVIDIA	24%
Cadence Design Systems	24%
ASML	22%

We can infer that a company with a consistently high return on capital and a consistently high margin has both pricing power and other competitive advantages. Qualitative research into the companies with these financial properties reveals the parts of their business models that they have in common.

The above list features a number of tech companies that have in recent years transitioned to the software-as-a-service business model. These include Microsoft and the accounting software provider Intuit. Similarly, companies like MSCI and Factset are operating a similar business model by providing data-as-a-service. What makes these business models so resilient is the fact that business critical services are being provided to corporate clients and are underpinned by licences, contracts and automatic renewals. This creates a predictable and recurring revenue stream that is unlikely to dry up, at least in the short- to medium-term. Switching from one service provider to another is often costly and time consuming for the corporate client, meaning that many software-as-a-service companies benefit from robust client retention.

The above list also features a number of monopolies and duopolies. The credit rating agencies, S&P Global and Moody's, are essentially a duopoly. Together they are the leading providers of credit ratings for fixed income securities, such as bonds. While they are not the only credit rating agencies, together they have the market share and 90% of the world's debt has a credit rating from either Moody's or S&P. The business model of the credit rating agencies benefits from two types of protection. Firstly, stringent regulation provides a barrier to entry. If you want to start a credit rating agency, you will be met with a wide range of legal requirements that have to be complied with at great cost. Secondly, both S&P and Moody's benefit from switching costs. Borrowers looking for a cheaper credit rating from one of the smaller competitors will be met with increased borrowing costs in the form of a higher interest rate on their debt. This can typically be between 30 - 50 basis points higher. This means even if a competitor were to offer its services for free, borrowers would still want to buy credit ratings from Moody's and S&P.

Another duopoly featured in the list are the credit card companies, Visa and Mastercard, who together are the world's largest payment processes. Visa processes over $10 trillion in transactions each year, while Mastercard does close to $6 trillion. As consumer spending around the world grows and digital payments replace cash, Visa and Mastercard are in a position to benefit from significant long-term trends and structural changes. They have essentially positioned themselves as a toll booth on global spending. While both have established brands recognised around the world, they have also created near-impossible to replicate payment networks consisting of thousands of financial institutions, millions of merchants and billions of card users. Therefore, this duopoly of payment processors enjoys a formidable barrier to entry.

Like the payment companies, financial exchanges (such as the London Stock Exchange and the Intercontinental Exchange who own the NYSE) benefit from network effects. This is one of the strongest competitive advantages a company can have. In the previously mentioned Morningstar paper, the authors demonstrated that network effects are not only rare, they are also highly resilient. Networks are hard to create and hard to destroy. The network effect is best observed in marketplaces. An increasing number of buyers attracts an increasing number of sellers, and vice versa. In the context of financial exchanges, as more buyers and sellers use the exchange, the bid-ask spread tightens prompting their order book to deepen. This creates a virtuous cycle for all market participants. Listed exchanges can be found in most developed markets, such as the Deutsche Borse in Germany, the ASX in Australia, the NZX in New Zealand and Euronext in Europe. There are even specialised exchanges, such as the Nasdaq for tech stocks, MarketAxess for credit markets, CME for derivatives and CBOE for options.

Healthcare companies, like the Danish company Novo Nordisk, typically benefit from a range of intangible assets. These take the form of patents, regulatory licences and brands. Patents are essentially a legal monopoly. While they form an important legal protection, they can expire and can also be revoked. High quality healthcare companies also benefit from the arguably more important intangible asset of having a trusted brand. Even if a company like Novo Nordisk saw all its patents expire, the trust that it has created with its customers is not only hard to replicate, it also means that their customers happily pay a premium for the quality of what's being sold to them.

Companies in the luxury goods industry, such as Hermes and LVMH, are also high margin businesses. But it is their brands alone that creates their pricing power. There are no switching costs or networks in play, just scarcity created through high prices that contributes to the perception of exclusivity. The brands owned by the luxury good conglomerates are typically over a century old, which is a business feature impossible to recreate overnight. Luxury has also proven itself, perhaps surprisingly, to be somewhat resilient during a recession. For example, LVMH reported growth during both the global financial crisis and the recent pandemic.

Finally, the above list features a number of companies in the semiconductor industry, such as Texas Instruments (the analog chip developer), Cadence Design Systems (provider of semiconductor design software) and ASML. High demand for semiconductors is being driven by growth in consumer electronics, smartphones, computers, the cloud and electric vehicles. ASML is often described as being one of the world's most important companies. It has a resilient business and is a vital cog in the tech machine. They are the only company that sells extreme ultra-violet (EUV) lithography machines. These machines are essential in the process of manufacturing the latest semiconductors. For a competitor to reproduce ASML's EUV machine and create their own version, they would need a huge investment of capital, time and customer partnerships in order to source the required technological knowledge and expertise and to even come remotely close to replicating what ASML is doing. This makes their barrier to entry extremely high. ASML's products are relied on and used by every major semiconductor manufacturer, including Intel, Samsung and the Taiwan Semiconductor Manufacturing Company (TSMC). Interestingly, many of ASML's customers are also ASML shareholders, further supporting their strong market position.

The importance of qualitative analysis

While the preceding chapters have demonstrated the importance of high FCF per share growth, high FCF returns on capital and high FCF margins, the above case studies should also demonstrate the importance of qualitative analysis. Strong financial metrics allow us to infer that a company has a resilient business, but it is also important that we support our inferences with an understanding of the business models of each potential investment. Set out below are a series of questions to help you get started with your qualitative research:

Relationship with suppliers

- What goods and services is the company buying?

- Who is providing these goods and services?

- Are there any risks to the supply chain?

Relationship with buyers

- How is the company adding value to what it is buying?

- What is the company selling? Goods or services? High-end or mass market?

— Who is the company selling to? Other companies or direct to consumers?

— Is demand for their goods and services increasing or decreasing?

— How predictable and recurring is the company's revenues? Are they backed by licences, contracts, automatic renewal, etc.?

— Are there new markets the company can enter to propel its growth?

— What has happened historically when the company has raised its prices? Were sales unaffected?

— What has happened historically to the company's sales during a recession?

Relationship with competitors and the economy

— Who is the company competing with? Is it a monopoly, in a duopoly or are there a range of competitors in the market?

— Is the company exposed to commodity prices and interest rates?

— In what ways is this company resilient and competitive?

Chapter 5:
Valuation

Market value and intrinsic value

Every minute of every business day the market provides investors with share prices. Multiplying a company's share price by the total number of shares a company has issued calculates the market value for the company as a whole. This is also known as the market capitalisation and it represents the amount of money you would need if you wanted to buy the entire company. But as an investor how do you know you're not overpaying?

That's where valuation comes in. There are a number of different methods for calculating valuation. Essentially the process is calculating what you think the intrinsic value of the company is and then comparing the calculated intrinsic value to what the market value actually is. If you think the company is worth more than the market does, then you may have an attractive investment.

Valuation principles

Before we get to the methods for calculating a company's value, it's best to start with two important valuation principles.

The first valuation principle is that a high valuation does not mean you are overpaying. Quality can be expensive. Similarly, a low valuation does not mean something is cheap. Low quality is often cheap for a reason. It is important that investors only focused on owning high quality assets first consider the quality of what they are buying, before assessing valuation. That is why the chapter on valuation comes after the chapters on growth, return on capital and pricing power. MSCI provides indices that capture companies that have high returns on capital (MSCI World Quality), high growth rates (MSCI World Growth) and cheap valuations (MSCI World Value). The following table shows that from 2012 - 2022, it was the companies that are high quality and growing that outperformed the market (MSCI World), not those that were cheap. This is possibly due to the value index being underweight quality growth stocks, owing to the premium that the market often charges for owning these companies.

Index	Annualised Return (2012 - 2022)
MSCI World Quality	11.1%
MSCI World Growth	9.9%
MSCI World	9.4%
MSCI World Value	8.6%

The second valuation principle is that you can still pay an expensive price and make a significant return. There are numerous historic examples of where investors could have paid expensive valuations and still made significantly high returns. This is because valuations are moments in time snapshots of moving objects. Imagine a photograph of sprinters taken halfway through a race. While the photo captures the positions of each runner at a specific moment in time, it does not reveal each runner's speed, whether they were getting faster or slowing down, how much energy they had left and who won the race. Similarly the market's valuation does not tell you how fast a company is growing, how predictable the company's revenues are, their ability to raise prices, whether it has new markets to enter and whether it can protect itself from economic cycles. There are plenty of examples in sport of teams and athletes that are behind making spectacular comebacks. There are also plenty of examples in business of beaten down companies making equally spectacular comebacks. While share price reflects the market's valuation at a specific moment in time, it does not tell you what's going to happen in the company's future.

Measures of value

Valuation essentially is a comparative exercise. It involves comparing the market's external value of the company with something internal to the business. For most investors, this means comparing the company's market value with its earnings to calculate the price-to-earnings ratio (P/E ratio). If a company's share price is $100 and it makes $2 in earnings per share, then the company's P/E ratio is 50 (100/2). Another way of understanding the ratio is that if earnings remain stagnant at $2 per share per year, then it would take 50 years for the company to earn what you paid for the shares.

The P/E ratio can be inversed to calculate the earnings yield. So $2 of earnings and a $100 share price also results in a 2% earnings yield (2/100). Another way of understanding this is that for every $100 invested in the company, $2 of earnings will be generated (again assuming earnings stay stagnant at $2 per share per year).

As we have already discussed, earnings can be massaged, and therefore a more robust approach to valuation is comparing the company's free cash flow to its market capitalisation to calculate the FCF yield. A company that generates $2 in FCF per share and has a share price of $100 will have a FCF yield of 2% (2/100). So for every $100 invested in the company, it returns $2 in cash.

As we also discussed earlier, the measurement of free cash flow can be distorted by stock-based compensation (SBC). This is because under the Generally accepted accounting principles (GAAP), SBC can end up being included in the calculation of free cash flow. It is therefore important to be aware of whether SBC is included in the FCF calculation and to subtract it where necessary, to ensure comparisons are made on a like-for-like for basis, i.e. not comparing the FCF+SBC yield of one company with the FCF-SBC yield of another.

Quality of free cash flow

While it is tempting to say that companies trading on a FCF yield of 4% have a more attractive valuation than companies trading at 2%, such a conclusion only focuses on the market's current valuation and does not consider the quality of the cash flows being valued. A company trading at a 2% FCF yield may have faster growth, a better quality underlying business, less exposure to economic cycles and low levels of debt on its balance sheet. The company trading at a 4% FCF yield may have slower growth, a shrinking market share, exposure to commodity prices and high amounts of debt on its balance sheet. Given that choice, it would make more sense for the investor to consider the company trading at 2%. Therefore, FCF yields cannot be considered in isolation.

In the following table both Company A and B generate $2.00 of FCF per share. Company A manages to grow its FCF at 20% per year, while Company B only manages to grow its FCF at 2% per year. While at first Company A is trading at twice the valuation of Company B (a 2% yield compared to a 4% yield in year 0), the forward FCF yield 5 years later is higher for Company A than Company B (4.98% compared to 4.42% in year 5). This is because over the long-term a high FCF growth rate means that the valuation is actually more attractive than it first appears.

Year	Company A			Company B		
	FCF per share	Share Price	FCF Yield	FCF per share	Share Price	FCF Yield
0	$2.00	$100	2.00%	$2.00	$50	4.00%
1	$2.40	$100	2.40%	$2.04	$50	4.08%
2	$2.88	$100	2.88%	$2.08	$50	4.16%
3	$3.46	$100	3.46%	$2.12	$50	4.24%
4	$4.15	$100	4.15%	$2.16	$50	4.33%
5	$4.98	$100	**4.98%**	$2.21	$50	**4.42%**

Ideally valuation should be a comparative exercise where you compare the relative valuations of high quality companies with high FCF growth rates. The following table sets out the FCF yields at the time of writing (December 2022) for a subset of high quality companies that have grown their FCF by over 15% per year over the last 5 years. The wide range of valuations (1.3% to 5.0%) demonstrates that there are often value opportunities among the universe of high quality companies.

Company	FCF yield	5yr FCF CAGR
Diasorin	5.0%	18%
ASML	4.2%	52%
Qualys	4.2%	29%
Visa	4.2%	18%
Constellation Software	3.6%	21%
Microsoft	3.5%	17%
Mastercard	3.2%	18%

TechnologyOne	3.2%	28%
MSCI	2.8%	21%
Cadence Design Systems	2.5%	22%
S&P Global	2.2%	22%
Mettler Toledo	2.1%	23%
NVIDIA	1.3%	41%

What influences share prices?

When you see that a company's share price has steadily gone up over time, the first reaction should be to question whether the share price growth was driven by free cash flow growth or a change in the market's valuation.

Cadence Design Systems	2012	2022	Growth
Share price	$13.51	$163.43	12x
FCF per share	$1.00	$3.96	4x
FCF yield	7.4%	2.4%	3x

The above table provides an example from Cadence Design Systems, the provider of semiconductor design software. From 2012 - 2022 their share price grew 12-fold, while free cash flow only grew 4-fold. It was the simultaneous 3-fold increase in the company's valuation that allowed its share price to outpace its FCF growth (3x4=12). A key conclusion from this exercise is that it reveals that Cadence's share price was driven more by internal growth than the external change in valuation. For many early stage companies, share price growth is often driven more by the change in the market's demand than the company's growth.

The following table describes three hypothetical companies. Each company grew its share price 6-fold. However, each company achieved this through different routes. Company A grew its free cash flows, Company B grew its valuation and Company C grew both. In reality it is Company C that reflects most quality growth companies. This example also demonstrates the important fact that any share price change can be understood by the growth of a company's free cash flow and the change in its valuation. Share price returns are ultimately driven by the change in valuation and growth. Stocks enjoying attractive valuations coupled with strong growth prospects have the potential for both increases in the valuation combined with growth in FCF to work together to create share price growth. That's why growth and valuation must be considered side by side. While a change in valuation can be significant, a company's growth can last for decades, hence why growth is the more important factor here.

	Company A	Company B	Company C
FCF growth:	6x	1x	2x
Valuation growth:	1x	6x	3x
Share price growth:	6x	6x	6x

It is therefore important to consider what it is that actually influences a company's share price. Ultimately it comes down to supply and demand, with the market's demand for a company's share being driven by:

1. <u>The market's view of the company's growth prospects</u>. This involves the market pricing in the company's actual historic earnings, the estimates of its future earnings and its competitive advantages.

2. <u>The market's view of the economy</u>. Company's don't exist in a vacuum, they exist as part of the wider economy. The market's valuation will price in economic factors such as inflation, employment, financial stability, public health and war. Changes in the earnings yield of the S&P 500 and the value of a volatility index, such as the VIX, are both useful indicators of the market's view of the economy and equities.

3. <u>The market's ability to invest</u>. Even if the market views a company and the economy favourably, the market can still be limited by its own ability to invest. The activity of central banks in setting the monetary supply, through interest rates and quantitative easing, also strongly influence share prices. Interest rates are often described as gravity for share prices. This is because a long-term low interest rate supports high valuations, while a long-term high interest rate suppresses valuations.

Bringing it all together

It can seem like there's a lot to consider when trying to come to a view on a company's valuation. However, valuation is not an exact science. The following chart shows the share price of McDonald's over the last several decades. It demonstrates that high quality growth companies more often than not provide suitable entry points for long-term investors on a frequent basis. This is why it is often said that "there is rarely a bad time to buy a compounding machine".

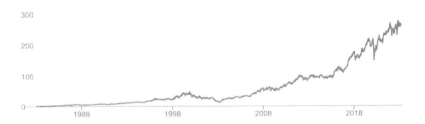

In closing, investors should focus primarily on the quality of a company's business, the resilience of its cash flows and the advantages it has over its competition. As long as these remain in place and you're prepared to be a long-term shareholder, the valuation you enter in, will more often than not, be of little consequence. Comparing the FCF yields of high quality companies, should help reveal the value opportunities that sit within the investment universe of high quality companies.

Chapter 6:
Intelligent Portfolio Construction

Picking companies is not enough. Once an investor is confident that they have found a high quality company trading at an attractive price, they then need to decide how that company is going to fit into their portfolio. Should it be their largest position or should they start off small? Should they sell an investment to make room? And at what point should they sell?

Imagine a situation where you are forced to invest all your money and the money of your closest friends and family into your portfolio. You are only allowed to select a few investments, no more than 20, and you are forbidden from buying or selling anything for at least the next 5 years. Such circumstances would incentivise you to only invest in safe, low risk companies that you would be happy putting your money and other peoples in for a long period of time. The overall effect would be that you become a concentrated, buy-and-hold investor focused on high quality companies. Assuming you take this approach, academic research actually suggests that you would do quite well. That's because research suggests that concentrated fund managers and long-term fund managers that trade infrequently outperform.

What works in investing?

Conventional wisdom suggests that investors should not put all their eggs in one basket and instead they should have a well diversified portfolio across not just geographies and sectors, but also across market capitalisation, business maturity and valuation. Academic findings actually suggest that diversification has limitations. As we have already seen, certain sectors have stronger fundamentals and better market performance than others. It's likely that adding airlines and banks to your portfolio will actually deteriorate the portfolio's quality and compromise its long-term performance, rather than benefit it through diversification.

What a lot of investors don't appreciate is that it is possible, in certain instances, to hold a single company and to still have a diversified portfolio. This is because some companies are themselves highly diversified with revenues generated across multiple business lines and multiple geographies. L'Oreal, for example, despite being listed in France, generates just 32% of its revenue from Europe, compared to 25% from North America and 31% from North Asia. It also owns several billion dollar brands, such as Garnier, Maybelline and Vichy. Similarly the fashion company, LVMH, while being a single company, is actually a conglomerate owning a range of brands including Christian Dior, Moët, Givenchy, TAG Heuer and Bulgari. The consumer goods companies, such as Procter & Gamble, Unilever, Nestle, Coca-Cola, PepsiCo and Colgate-Palmolive, are also fantastic examples of companies with diversified revenues across business lines and geographies. P&G operates the billion dollar businesses Tide, Pantene and Gilette, and generates around one third of its revenue from emerging markets. The diversification of the revenue streams of your investments is an important factor when considering the overall diversification of your portfolio.

The 2006 research paper "Fund Managers Who Take Big Bets", found that concentrated fund managers, so managers of portfolios consisting of a low number of companies, actually outperformed their more diversified counterparts. Similarly research has shown that the benefits of diversification decay quickly. A portfolio of less than 5 stocks has a fairly significant amount of portfolio risk, while a portfolio with 20-25 equal-sized positions sees portfolio risk eliminated, with only the wider market risk inherent to equities remaining.

The 1998 research paper "Do Investors Trade Too Much?" analysed 10,000 brokerage accounts to compare whether the securities that investors buy outperform those they sell. Surprisingly they found that it was actually the securities that were sold that outperformed those that were bought, highlighting that investors are indeed prone to trading too much and suggesting that often the best investment decision is to do nothing.

The above evidence suggests that 20-25 high quality companies held for the long-term is probably all that the average investor needs to be diversified and to outperform. This approach ensures that investments are given the time required to compound their value. The lesson here is: don't interrupt compounding unnecessarily.

When should an investor sell?

We established in the preceding chapters the importance of only investing in companies that have high free cash flow per share, high returns on capital, high margins and an attractive free cash flow yield. Portfolios should therefore be constructed to maximise for these four investment ratios. Consequently, any investment decision, whether it is to sell or to buy, should be for the sole purpose of maximising the quality of the portfolio. Compounding takes time. As long as a company remains high quality then there is unlikely to be a need to sell. Trading should be for the sole purpose of maximising the quality of your portfolio.

Finding the best investments through scoring

Having established the four key ratios to look for in a company, we can now move on to considering how to evaluate potential investments. One approach is to have a threshold for each of the four ratios and then to score each company based on whether it meets the threshold. The following table provides a score for a large number of high quality growth companies. 10 year averages (2012 - 2022) were used to ensure that only long-term value creators and price setters were captured. For FCF return on capital, FCF margin and FCF compound annual growth rate the threshold was taken as 15%. For the linearity of FCF growth rate, the R-Squared was taken as 0.85. In the table a blob has been inserted into each cell where the threshold is met. The table is sorted so that companies that score 4/4 are at the top and those that score 0/4 are at the bottom. Interestingly, the annualised share price return over the same 10 year period for companies scoring a 4 was 26%, while for those scoring a 3 the return was 20% and for those scoring 2 or less the return was 18%. So clearly there is some merit in scoring investments based on these metrics.

Company	Score	10yr avg. FCF ROC (%)	10yr avg. FCF Margin (%)	10yr FCF CAGR (%)	10yr FCF Linearity (Rsq)
Adobe	4	•	•	•	•
Alphabet	4	•	•	•	•
Constellation Software	4	•	•	•	•
Fair Isaac	4	•	•	•	•
Hermes	4	•	•	•	•
KLA	4	•	•	•	•
Lam Research	4	•	•	•	•
Mettler Toledo	4	•	•	•	•
MSCI	4	•	•	•	•
Nemetschek	4	•	•	•	•
NVIDIA	4	•	•	•	•
PayPal	4	•	•	•	•
Qualys	4	•	•	•	•
S&P Global	4	•	•	•	•
TechnologyOne	4	•	•	•	•
Veeva Systems	4	•	•	•	•
ASML	3	•	•	•	
Automatic Data Processing	3	•	•		•
Cadence	3	•	•		•
Descartes Systems	3		•	•	•
Diasorin	3	•	•		•
Edwards Lifesciences	3	•	•	•	
Exponent	3	•	•		•
Factset	3	•	•		•
IDEXX	3	•		•	•
Infosys	3	•	•		•
Intuit	3	•	•		•
Jack Henry	3	•	•		•
MarketAxess	3	•	•		•
Mastercard	3	•	•		•
Microsoft	3	•	•		•
Monolithic Power Systems	3		•	•	•

Moodys	3	•	•		•
Novo Nordisk	3	•	•		•
Paychex	3	•	•		•
Paycom	3	•		•	•
Texas Instruments	3	•	•		•
Verisign	3	•	•		•
Visa	3	•	•		•
Zebra Technologies	3	•		•	•
Zoetis	3		•	•	•
Amazon	2			•	•
Analog Devices	2		•		•
ANSYS	2		•		•
Aspen Tech	2		•		•
Autodesk	2	•	•		
CSL	2		•	•	
Dassault Systèmes	2		•		•
Expeditors International	2	•			•
Fisher & Paykel	2	•		•	
Heico	2		•		•
ICE	2		•		•
LSE	2		•	•	
LVMH	2			•	•
Nasdaq	2		•		•
Open Text	2		•		•
Procter & Gamble	2		•		•
Qualcomm	2	•	•		
Recordati	2		•	•	
Thermo Fisher	2		•		•
Amphenol	1				•
Danaher	1		•		
Estee Lauder	1	•			
L'Oreal	1				•
Sartorius Stedim	1			•	
Synopsys	1		•		
Costco	0				

Informed decision making through ranking

There's a lot that can be factored into a decision to buy or sell a stock. Like scoring, informed decisions can also be made through ranking your options.

The following table sets out the portfolio size, the FCF yield and the FCF CAGR of 23 companies in a portfolio (see columns 2-4). A rank has been assigned to each company for each of these three metrics (see columns 5-7). As Microsoft is the largest position it has a portfolio size rank of 1, while the smallest position - NVIDIA - has a rank of 23. As Amazon has the lowest FCF yield it has a rank of 1, while Diasorin's high FCF yield means it has a rank of 23. As Amazon has the lowest FCF growth rate it has a rank of 1, while ASML's high FCF growth rate means it has a rank of 23. We can then total up these three ranks to create a total rank. The table has been sorted by this total rank. This brings Qualys, ASML and Diasorin to the top. These are all companies that have high FCF growth rates, attractive valuations and currently occupy small positions within the portfolio. This suggests that any allocation of capital should be made towards these companies, as this would help maximise the FCF growth rate and valuation of the portfolio as a whole. Qualys notably didn't appear as a top position for any of the three ranks, yet it has the highest total rank overall, demonstrating the power of totalling up multiple ranks.

Holding	Portfolio Size	FCF yield	FCF CAGR	Portfolio Rank	Yield Rank	CAGR Rank	Total Rank
Qualys	2.2%	4.2%	27%	21	22	20	63
ASML	2.8%	4.2%	33%	17	21	23	61
Diasorin	2.2%	5.0%	14%	22	23	12	57
Constellation Software	5.1%	3.6%	28%	10	17	21	48
NVIDIA	1.9%	1.3%	29%	23	2	22	47
TechnologyOne	3.0%	3.2%	16%	15	12	15	42
Visa	6.8%	4.2%	24%	2	20	19	41
Texas Instruments	3.8%	4.0%	10%	14	19	7	40
Paychex	2.9%	3.6%	9%	16	18	5	39
Automatic Data	2.3%	3.5%	8%	20	16	3	39
Novo Nordisk	2.6%	2.8%	10%	18	10	8	36
FactSet	2.6%	3.3%	8%	19	13	4	36
Intuit	5.1%	3.5%	12%	9	15	11	35
Mettler Toledo	4.8%	2.1%	17%	12	4	17	33
Cadence	4.9%	2.5%	14%	11	7	13	31
MSCI	6.1%	2.8%	16%	5	9	16	30
Mastercard	6.3%	3.2%	15%	4	11	14	29
Moody's	4.1%	2.2%	11%	13	6	9	28
SPGI	6.6%	2.2%	21%	3	5	18	26
Microsoft	7.0%	3.5%	12%	1	14	10	25
Costco	5.2%	1.4%	10%	8	3	6	17
L'Oreal	6.1%	2.7%	8%	6	8	2	16
Amazon	5.5%	-3.1%	0%	7	1	1	9

Time-weighted return (TWR)

We're now approaching the end of the book. We've covered how to create a shortlist of potential investments, how to evaluate that shortlist based on four financial metrics and how to use scoring and ranking to inform your investment decision making. Having put together a portfolio of high quality companies, all that's left to do is sit back and monitor its performance. It can be difficult to calculate the return of a portfolio when there are numerous inflows and outflows of cash. You can't simply subtract the starting balance from the end balance, as your return will also include cash that was added to the portfolio. This is where time-weighted return comes in. It allows you to account for your portfolio's inflows and outflows when calculating the compound rate of growth of your portfolio.

An example is set out in the following table. You start the year with $10,000. At the end of January your portfolio grows by 5% to $10,500. At the end of February your portfolio has grown again, this time by 4.8%, to $11,000. In March you decide to add $1,000 to your portfolio. Therefore, while you started with $11,000, your inflow means you actually started with $12,000. You also end March with $12,000, meaning your portfolio didn't grow during this month. In April your portfolio drops in value to $11,000, representing a -8.3% loss. In May you decide to withdraw $500 from your portfolio. Therefore, while you started the month with $11,000, you actually started with $10,500. You end May with $11,000 again, meaning that your portfolio has grown by 4.8%. You end June with $12,000, meaning your portfolio grew by 9.1% over the month and by 15.2% over the first half of the year.

Month	Start ($)	Flow ($)	Actual Start ($)	End ($)	TWR	%
January	10,000	0	10,000	10,500	0.050	5.0%
February	10,500	0	10,500	11,000	0.048	4.8%
March	11,000	1,000	12,000	12,000	0.000	0.0%
April	12,000	0	12,000	11,000	-0.083	-8.3%
May	11,000	-500	10,500	11,000	0.048	4.8%
June	11,000	0	11,000	12,000	0.091	9.1%
				YTD:	0.152	15.2%

To calculate the time-weighted return for each period, you simply need to divide the End value by the Actual Start value and then subtract 1. So for January this is:

$$10,500 / 10,000 - 1 = 0.05$$

TWR is a fraction, which can then be expressed as a percentage. In this instance it's 5.0%. Having calculated the TWR for each period, we can then calculate the year to date (YTD) return. To do this we simply add 1 to each TWR value, then multiply each value, before finally subtracting 1. So in this example we simply calculate the following:

$$(0.050 + 1) * (0.048 + 1) * (0.000 + 1) * (-0.083 + 1) *$$
$$(0.048 + 1) * (0.091 + 1) - 1 = 0.152$$

Again, this fraction can be expressed as a percentage, to reveal that the year to date performance of the portfolio is 15.2%. While the time periods used in the above example are months, the same approach could be used for days or years. You can then compare your return to other investors or the market.

Having screened and filtered thousands of potential investments, and evaluated each investment based on their quality and valuation, it is ultimately your portfolio's time-weighted return that matters.

Chapter 7:
Quality Companies Worth Analysing

Just in case you need some inspiration before putting this book down, included below are some generally accepted high quality businesses from around the world. This is obviously not an exhaustive list. It is meant for research purposes only. Hopefully this will provide a useful place to start in your analysis.

North America

Canada

- Alimentation Couche-Tard

- Canadian National Railway

- Canadian Pacific Railway

- Constellation Software

- Descartes Systems

- Terravest Capital

- Waste Connections

USA

- A O Smith

- Abbott Laboratories

- Adobe

- Alphabet

- Amazon

- Amphenol

- Analog Devices

- Apple

- Automatic Data Processing

- Broadcom

- Cadence Design Systems

- Coca-Cola

- Colgate-Palmolive

- Cooper Companies

- Copart

- Costco

- Danaher

- Edwards Lifesciences

- Eli Lilly

- Estee Lauder

- Equifax

- Factset Research

- Fair Isaac

- Heico

- Home Depot

- IDEXX

- Intercontinental Exchange

- Intuit

- Intuitive Surgical

- Johnson & Johnson

- KLA Corp

- Lam Research

- Mastercard

- McDonalds

- Mettler Toledo

- Microsoft
- Moodys
- MSCI
- Nasdaq
- Nike
- NVIDIA
- Old Dominion Freight Line
- Paychex
- Pepsico
- Pool Corp
- Procter & Gamble
- Roper Technologies
- S&P Global
- Sherwin-Williams
- Synopsys
- Texas Instruments
- Thermo Fisher
- TransDigm Group
- Ulta Beauty

- UnitedHealth

- Verisign

- Visa

- Waste Management

- Zoetis

<u>Europe</u>

Belgium

- Lotus Bakeries

Denmark

- Chemometec

- CHR Hansen

- Coloplast

- DSV

- Genmab

- Novo Nordisk

- Novozymes

- Simcorp

Finland

- Kesko
- Kone
- Marimekko
- Neste
- Orion
- Revenio

France

- Air Liquide
- Dassault Systemes
- EssilorLuxottica
- Euronext
- Hermes
- Kering
- L'Oreal
- LVMH
- Pernod Ricard
- Remy Cointreau
- Robertet

- Safran

- Sanofi

- Sartorius Stedim Biotech

- Teleperformance

Netherlands

- Adyen

- ASM international

- ASML

- DSM

- Topicus

Germany

- Adidas

- ATOSS Software

- Bechtle

- Carl Zeiss Meditec

- Deutsche Boerse

- Fielmann

- Linde

- Mensch und Maschine

- Nemetschek

- Puma

- Rational

- SAP

- Sartorius

- Symrise

Italy

- Amplifon

- Davide Campari-Milano

- Diasorin

- Ferrari

- Moncler

- Recordati

Spain

- Amadeus IT

- Inditex

Sweden

- Addtech

- Assa Abloy

- Atlas Copco

- BioGaia

- CellaVision

- Evolution

- Fortnox

- Hexagon

- Investment AB Latour

- Investor AB

- Lifco

- Nibe Industrier

- Sectra

Switzerland

- Belimo

- Geberit

- Givaudan

- Lindt

- Logitech
- Lonza
- Nestlé
- Richemont
- Roche
- Schindler
- Sika
- Sonova
- Straumann

UK

- AG Barr
- Ashtead Group
- BAE Systems
- Cerillion
- Diageo
- Diploma
- Experian
- Halma
- Judges Scientific

- LSE

- Reckitt Benckiser

- Rightmove

- Spirax Sarco

- Unilever

- YouGov

Asia-Pacific

Australia

- ASX

- Cochlear

- CSL

- Resmed

- TechnologyOne

China / Hong Kong

- Alibaba

- ANTA Sports

- Foshan Haitian Flavouring

- Hong Kong Exchanges and Clearing

- Kweichow Moutai

- Li Ning

- NetEase

- Tencent

Japan

- Advantest

- Hoya Corp

- Kao Corp

- Keyence

- Nintendo

- Shiseido

India

- Asian Paints

- Hindustan Unilever

- Honeywell Automation

- Housing Development Finance

- Infosys

- Nestlé India

- Page Industries

- Pidilite Industries

New Zealand

- Fisher & Paykel

- Mainfreight

- NZX

Taiwan

- Taiwan Semiconductor Manufacturing Company

Made in the USA
Monee, IL
20 February 2023

28343730R00049